The Peculiar Path of Peter Polowy

A Story of War, Hope, Love, and Loss

I0158476

h. Alton Jones

54 Candles Publishing
Scottsdale, Arizona

To those who don't know who you are, that don't know your roots, your history, or from whence you came, this book is for you. It serves as an example for those tempted to give up hope. Keep looking. Keep searching. Don't give up. The hunt begins by looking inward for you are those who walked before you. Don't waste any more time. The hour is late. It is slipping away.

Introduction

This is a work of historical-fiction. That is not to say it isn't true and accurate. Quite the contrary. Many hours of research went into studying the history of the period in Eastern Europe and eastern Pennsylvania covered in this book. Many hundreds, if not thousands, or hours went into the genealogical research necessary to discover these heretofore unknown relationships.

However, the fact is that in some of the situations described herein, a small amount of creative fiction was necessary to bring all the pieces together. Every effort was made to verify the circumstance discussed. If an element of literary license was necessary to bring the story together, it was based upon the known facts. Assumptions were realistic.

For the most part, the book tells the very real story of the Polowy family and its journey from war-ravaged Ukraine to becoming Americans and living that dream. The Polowys epitomize the epic journey that made America what it is today. Their journey can also serve as an example of what needs to be done to keep America on track.

Hard work, tenacity, persistence, honesty, and family combine with the attributes of remembering and honoring your family history to produce this story. The real authors of this tale are the generations of the Polowy family that spent their lives reaching higher and never giving up.

Chapter One

The numbness of the hard winter of 1899 was being chased from their bones by an early spring. Snow still lay in the shadows, but the sun was striping the cover from large patches of the Polowy farm in Probizhna. The trees held back their leaves, but buds were visible as temperatures rose into the low forties, the Polowy family looked ahead to another year in the western Ukraine.

Jacob and Anna Polowy, like the generations before them, were farmers. Their first-born son, Michael, had not yet celebrated his fifth birthday, but he was already learning the simple tasks of farm life helping his mother whenever he could. As spring heralded the arrival of new life, Anna was preparing to have her third child. Life on a Ukrainian farm wasn't a life of luxury. Anna would continue to work long days and into the evening hours taking care of her duties at home while Jacob cared for the chickens, a pig, a milk cow, and a lone plow-horse. He was preparing to till the fields for the spring planting of their staple crops, wheat, cabbage, carrots, potatoes, beats, onions, cucumbers, and beans. The farm was on a long strip of land about five acres in size. It had been bigger, but over the generations, it had been halved and halved again.

Despite the rural lifestyle of Probizhna, the houses fell one after another along the dirt lane. Each of the family farms amounted to a long, narrow strip of land. As you can see in the recent picture of Probizhna, it remains that way today. Neighbors were close together and enjoyed a lot of social interaction, sharing, and cooperation. Families shared pasture land for the grazing animals and helped other neighbors when needs arose. The sense of "community" was strong.

Most residents looked to the Greek Catholic Church as the center of their lives, both socially and spiritually. Residents that were aligned with the Polish political world were followers of the Roman Catholic Church. Language was similarly divided between the Polish language and Ruthenian, the Ukrainian dialect of the Russian language. The groups interfaced on a regular basis, but they didn't always see eye-to-eye. Jacob and Anna saw the Russian language as their mother tongue. The Greek Catholic Church was their family's long-standing preference. They were Ukrainians.

Jacob, Anna, and young Michael lived in a small house with a thatch roof. It was no bigger than twenty by thirty feet with one enclosed bedroom for Jacob and Anna, a cooking area with a table, a couple of wooden seats, and two small benches. Young Michael slept in a corner of the open area opposite the kitchen area. Foods were stored in the root-cellar to get them through the long and bitter winters.

A second thatch roofed building served as the barn where their limited farm equipment was housed and where the animals could shelter from the harsh weather. With warmer days, the ice on the nearby stream was breaking up and water levels were rising, just as they did every spring. 1899 dawned a year of hope and optimism, despite the dark developments on the political fronts.

Probizhna sits less than ten miles west of Husyatyn, a city of some importance built within the horseshoe bend of the Zbruch River. With nearly seven thousand residents, Husyatyn was one of the bigger cities in the area. The population was predominantly Jewish and leaned Ukrainian/Russian politically. Poles amounted to a small, but influential land-holding class in Husyatyn. The city sat on the Austria-Hungary border with the

Russian Empire and served as a significant milestone on the east-west trade route through the Ukraine.

In the years Jacob had a surplus of crops, he would take them to market in Husyatyn. The city was big enough to have some commerce and Jacob was able to make some money and pick up needed supplies. It was a long day, but it was some time away from the farm, almost a day of rest in a strenuous sort of way.

When the commercial demands were greater and Husyatyn wasn't big enough to have needed supplies or equipment, Jacob made the long trip to Ternopil forty or so miles northwest of Probizhna. The city had grown rapidly since the Galician Railway of Archduke Charles Louis had connected it with the capitol city of Lemberg in Austria-Hungary about twenty-five years earlier. Ternopil had about 25,000 residents in 1875, but by 1899, it had grown to more than 40,000. Like Husyatyn and many of the bigger cities in the region, it had a large Jewish population; on the order of one in five residents were Jewish. Poles and Ukrainians accounted for nearly equal numbers for the balance. It was the closest major city to Probizhna.

Lemberg, the Galician Railway hub, was the German name of the area's biggest metropolitan center when the Ukraine was a part of the Austria-Hungary (Hapsburg) empire. Lemberg's Russian and Polish name is Lviv. Today, it is the seventh largest city in the Ukraine. In 1899, Lviv (Lemberg) was home to universities, theaters, industry, and everything major cities had to offer.

At the turn of the century, the entire area consisting of what is today southeastern Poland and the western Ukraine was considered a quasi-independent entity called Galicia within the Austria-Hungary empire. In centuries past, it had been a part of Poland, Russia, Austria, Germany, it had been invaded and occupied by numerous groups including the Turks. Within a couple decades, it would be the possession of the Russians, the Germans, Poland, and the independent nation named Western

Ukrainian People's Republic. It's no wonder that genealogists that research people from the area of Probishna are initially confused when they discover their subjects claimed four or five different nations are their home countries. They could do that without ever leaving the house.

As the summer of 1899 wore on, the Polowy's crops began to ripen. Life was good, but there were dark clouds on the political horizon that caused Jacob and Anna to worry. As the growing season inched closer to harvest, Anna awoke early one morning to a sharp pain. The pains repeated themselves over the next three hours. The mid-wife was summoned and just before noon on Saturday, the fifth of August, the Polowy family had a new, albeit inexperienced, farm-hand. Peter Polowy arrived as the second son and third child of Jacob and Anna.

Peter was a normal sized, healthy, vigorous newborn with a head sparsely populated with dark hair. He was born at home as nearly all of the children were in Probizhna. Anna's labor was easier with the third child than it had been nearly five years earlier with her first. By the following day, Peter had been baptized and christened into the local Greek Catholic Church.

At the same time Anna was giving birth to Peter, a group of Ukrainian populist leaders were traveling to Lviv to meet and create the Ruthenian National Democratic Party. The NDP was a centrist group intent on breaking from the radical Ukrainians that advocated for political alignment with the Czarists in Russia. The NDP wanted Ukrainian unity and independence. Peter was born into the world that had always been a volatile mix of politics and conquest, but the struggles would increase as Peter grew from infant, to toddler, to child, adolescent and young man. Peter's future was destined to be tumultuous at best.

Chapter Two

In the absence of political strife, farm life involves long and hard days. Crops and animals don't run on calendars, don't have schedules, and don't concern themselves with yours. When the wild plants deliver their fruits, you're there to harvest the nuts, berries, and grapes on their schedules, not yours. That's the small world Peter Polowy knew when he learned to walk. He looked up to his older brother and Michael took Peter under his wing as often as possible.

When Peter was barely a year old, a man named Vladimir Lenin published a pamphlet named "What is to be done?" It ultimately precipitated the creation of the Bolshevik party in Russia. In retrospect, it seems ironic that event would later come to play an outsized role in the life of a boy whose greatest challenge at that time was collecting chicken eggs without breaking them.

When Peter was three years old, he became the "middle boy" when John Polowy was born in early May. As the boys grew, the farm took most, but not all, of their time. There were other boys on the nearby farms. They saw them in church and they spent plenty of time with them exploring the nearby forests and streams. Peter tended toward small for his age, but he made up for it with brashness. He feared little if anything. Heaven help the local bully that pushed Peter too far. He could, would, and did defend himself on more than a few occasions. Of course, in the unlikely event the bully prevailed, it was only a temporary triumph. With a brother five years older whose muscles were toned with hard work on the farm, the victories invariably fell to the Polowy clan.

Peter started school when he turned six. With a family whose lives were dependent upon the success of the farm, his attendance wasn't without fault. It was no surprise that Peter preferred hunting rabbits to being tapped on the knuckles by the teacher in school. Peter made it through the fifth grade before duties on the farm called for his full-time attention. At that point, education was a luxury; food was a necessity.

In part because of the closure of the border between Russia and Galicia along the Zbruch River near Probizhna, the economy began faltering. The increased political instability resulted in a substantial drop in the inflow of capital. Jobs became harder and harder to find. Meanwhile, at the University of Lviv, young students grew increasingly active politically and more militant. The ethnic Polish and the Ukrainian students became more fractious each advocating for independence. As the Ukrainians called for independence, the Poles attempted to limit their efforts. Relations were on a serious downhill slide at this point and a number of violent clashes broke out. Things continued to spiral out-of-control when in 1908, a Ukrainian student assassinated a high-ranking Polish Vicegerent. Meanwhile, Peter was pulling the weeds from the cabbage patch and milking the cow. Jacob, on the other hand, talked with his neighbors frequently about the ominous signs of trouble they saw coming.

Jacob and the family were salt-of-the-earth farmers. And they were Ukrainians. As talk of conflict ran rampant throughout the western Ukraine, including in Probizhna, Jacob felt a heightened sense of nationalism. He didn't know precisely what path life would take, but he did know that he had a family to feed and care for and he kept his nose to the grindstone. No one in the family looked up from their duties. Their only option was to keep working to feed themselves. They couldn't afford the luxury of looking too far into the future. The church provided them their view of eternity. Hunger gave them their view of today.

By 1912, with the economy spiraling downward, without the prospect of a job, and not content with life on the farm, 18-year-old Michael decided to follow in the footsteps of many of his countrymen. He managed to secure a passport and round up enough money to buy transportation from Probizhna to the United States. From Ellis Island, he went to stay with a friend in Lackawanna, Pennsylvania. The friend had assured him he could get a good paying job in the coal mines that were flourishing there. Michael wasted no time in going to work as a hard-coal miner making more than $1.00 per 10-hour day. He was living the dream.

Back on the farm, their world took a very dramatic turn on June 28, 1914 as did the lives of everyone in Probizhna, the Ukraine, and the world. Austrian Archduke Franz Ferdinand was executed. That triggered a series of events that led to the start of World War I. Peter was two weeks shy of his fifteenth birthday. From that day forward, Peter would be growing up fast, very, very, fast.

Chapter Three

Perhaps, this is a good time for a little summary. The western Ukraine was the heart of Galicia. Lviv (Lemberg) was the heart of the western Ukraine. Probizhna was a small farming community in the orbit of Lviv.

Roughly half the residents of the area had loyalties to their Polish roots. What is now known as Poland was part of the Austro-Hungarian Empire. Poland fell strongly in with one side of the conflict that became World War I along with Austria, Hungary, Germany, Bulgaria, and the Ottoman Empire, i.e., the Turks.

The other half of Galicia's residents remained loyal to their Ukrainian roots, i.e., the Russians. In the first World War, the Russians were allied with France, Great Britain, Italy, Japan, and the United States.

So here we are in a little farming town in the center of a region whose people are evenly split between the two sides in what was to become one of history's greatest conflagrations that would produce approximately forty-million casualties. Spoiler alert! This doesn't bode well for a fifteen-year-old farm boy.

Peter celebrated his fifteenth birthday still somewhat oblivious to the future he faced. Rumors fast circulating in Probizhna left everyone with a sense of foreboding, but Peter's youth made it more difficult for him to put the pieces together than it did for his father, Jacob.

The day after Peter's birthday, as the Russians were amassing a million troops in the east, the authorities from the Austro-Hungarian forces in Lviv arrived in Probizhna. They had been combing the area looking for Russophiles whose allegiances were with the Russians. The Polowys lived close to the border, spoke Russian, attended the church associated with the Russians. The authorities concluded the Polowys were potential adversaries. They were probably right.

Right or wrong, the authorities weren't taking any chances. Jacob and Peter were detained and taken to an Austrian internment camp in Thalerhof more than 500 miles to the west.

Less than a month later, the Battle of Galicia began. In anticipation of a planned attack by the Austro-Hungarian forces, the Russians had entered Galicia. More than two million troops faced off in one of the first brutal battles of the war. It raged for nearly a month. More than a half million combatants were killed or wounded. Communities were destroyed. The Russians prevailed convincingly. When the dust had settled, the Russians controlled Lviv.

Peter spent nearly three years in Thalerhof with 7,000 other Ukrainians with questioned loyalties. As a result of poor sanitation and a lack of nourishment, typhus, dysentery, and other diseases, less than half of the initial 7,000 survived to the end of the war. Those that did survive lived lives of forced labor in support of the German and Austrian war efforts.

Early in 1917, there was talk of forming an army consisting of those prisoners who vowed support for the Polish cause. Peter had mixed feelings before the war. When he learned that support of the Polish cause meant an exit from forced labor and certain death, it should surprise no one that Peter began leaning, at least publicly, toward the cause of Polish independence.

(In the photo, Peter is seen posing with his sister Barbara in Lviv in about 1920.)

On June 4th, the Polish Blue Army, also known as Haller's Army, was created. Peter was one of the first to volunteer. They were named the Polish Blue Army because their uniforms were donated by the French and were unmistakably blue. Initially, they were assigned to the "Western Front" in France and fought alongside the allied forces. But when all was quiet on the Western Front, the Polish Blues were moved east to the newly independent Poland.

Peter was on the train headed back much closer to home, a home that no longer existed. Although Probizhna itself hadn't seen the heaviest fighting, it was still dramatically impacted. Many of Peter's old friends and neighbors would never be seen again. The Probizhna of 1914 no longer existed.

With the signing of the Armistice in 1918, the people of the west Ukraine, under the banner of the NDP, formed an independent nation, The Western Ukrainian People's Republic. The allies sent Polish forces, most notably, the Blue Army into the Ukraine ostensibly to repel the Russian Bolsheviks who were now turning Russian upside-down. The Blues were instructed to not engage with the army of the newly formed Western Ukrainian People's Republic. But, boys will be boys. The animosities that existed before 1914 erupted and the Blues engaged with the Ukrainians in the Polish-Ukrainian War. By July of 1919, the Western Ukrainian People's Republic no longer existed as a political entity and the Poles had prevailed. Suspecting complicity with the Bolsheviks, some of the Polish Blues participated in incidents of anti-Jewish violence on the march through Galicia. The Polish Blue Army had repulsed the Bolsheviks and established the eastern border of the newly formed Poland as the Zbruch River, a short distance from the Polowy family farm.

Peter returned to Probizhna and found the farm abandoned. He looked out over the fields in which he had worked and played and thought about how much they had changed. His memories of the past there lingered like pieces of dreams after a heavy sleep. Everything was different. He left Probizhna nearly five years ago as a boy. He stood outside the house in which he was born as a battle-hardened young man. His family wasn't there. The farm was abandoned. He would never see his father again. He could have been conscripted by the Russian Army. He may have died in an Austrian internment camp. Peter would never know. Peter's return home was a most disheartening event. As he stood on the soil that had absorbed so many beads of his sweat and those of his family and ancestors, a tear ran down his cheek. It fell to the ground almost as if it was the ceremonial consecration of the end to his final visit home.

Chapter Four

Peter returned to his unit and served out his time with the Polish Blues. He scrimped and saved. He was motivated by the rare letter he received from his brother Michael who had now spent nearly ten years in America. He dreamed of the day when he could have a steady job, earn a living wage, and go to sleep at night without the sound of rifle and canon fire.

In November of 1922, Peter applied with the Polish authorities for his passport. It was granted. He purchased his train tickets for travel from Lviv, Poland with four connections over a thousand miles across Germany destined for the inland port of Antwerp, Belgium. On Friday, the 29th of December, 1922, a twenty-three-year-old man from Probizhna boarded the Star Lines ocean liner named Lapland. Peter Polowy would spend the next eleven days with over a thousand other dreamers looking toward a new life in America. They had a brief stop in Southampton, England to take on additional passengers before the bow was pointed west toward New York. Peter traveled as a "third class" (also known as steerage) passenger. It wasn't luxurious. They passed through one storm that gave him some cause for alarm, but for the most part, it was a smooth and relatively uneventful voyage. He had nearly two weeks to reflect on his life, past and future. He talked with others about memories of their past and dreams of their future.

(Peter's annotated passport after passing through Ellis Island.)

As the sun broke the horizon on Tuesday, January 9, 1923, Peter was on deck and watched in amazement as a strange object pierced the sea's placid surface and glistened in the early morning sun. As it slowly reached toward the sky, Peter could make out the shape of a torch of some kind. Finally, the face of a lady was looking toward him. Peter was arriving in America and the lady known as the Statue of Liberty beckoned him into the harbor. Before the sun set that cold day, Peter stood in front of a U.S. Customs agent on Ellis Island in the New York Harbor. On his entry document, the Customs agent wrote the destination Peter had given the translator: Mike Polowy, 8326 Scott Street, Olyphant, Pennsylvania. One more train ride and Peter would begin a new life far from the wars and strife he had lived through for the past ten years.

Peter lived for a time with his brother Michael, and his wife, Dorothy, and three young children until he got his feet on the ground. Peter's first order of business was to apply for a job at the Pennsylvania Coal Company's Underwood Colliery. Construction on the mine had begun the year Michael arrived and it was growing rapidly. Hundreds of immigrants from Poland, Russia, Scotland, Italy and other places traumatized from the events of World War I flocked to the east Pennsylvania coal mines. Labor was in short supply.

On his second full day as a resident of his new country, Peter reported for work on a cold, blustery winter day. His ability to speak English was all but non-existent, but there were enough other eastern European workers to help Peter communicate and begin to learn his new language.

Peter worked as an underground laborer mining anthracite coal. It was hard, dirty, dangerous, back-breaking work ten hours every day, six days per week. In exchange for his labors, he earned $9.00 per week. It worked out to about fifteen-cents per hour. With hard work and dedication, he would soon to be earning seventeen cents per hour and grossing more than $10 per week. Peter wasn't rubbing elbows with the Carnegies, but he had steady work and a living wage.

By 1923, Olyphant had become a "company town". The firm had built a "company store" where its workers formed a nearly captive audience. A small hospital had also been constructed for the mine workers. The company was also constructing "Underwood Village", an area near the mine with houses the company rented to its employees. Peter's brother, Michael, had been one of the first non-supervisor level employees to rent a house in the Village. Peter put his name on the list of those employees wanting a house.

In the meantime, Peter worked faithfully at the mine. Even though he was 5'7" and less than 150 pounds, Peter was a sinewy young man and could outperform nearly everyone in the mine. The demands for coal left him without much spare time, but Sundays found him with many of his Ukrainian expatriates at SS Cyril and Methodius Ukrainian Catholic Church. He worshipped there and was delighted to attend some of the social activities offered Sunday afternoons.

In addition to the social aspects of being a part of the church, it gave Peter an opportunity to practice his budding English. At a potluck dinner at the church in 1924, Peter practiced his English on a beautiful, nineteen-year-old lady. She found Peter more than attractive and engaging. Even though her parents had been born in the old world, she was born and raised in the area and her English skills were excellent. She offered to help Peter learn English and assured him practice would make perfect. Her name was Evelyn Fallat.

For the next forty-four years, Eva talked English with Peter. In 1927, they became Mr. and Mrs. Peter Polowy. He had found the love of his life. They moved into their new residence, a company house in the Underwood Village section of Olyphant. Peter worked for the coal mines of Olyphant until her retired in 1955.

Eleven months after they were married, Peter and Eva welcomed their first of three children into the world. Anna Mae Polowy was born on May 18, 1928. A little over a year later in October 1929, Michael Peter Polowy was born. It was more than five years later, Eugene was born. He died a month after his first birthday after contracting scarlet fever.

Peter and Eva dedicated their lives to providing a pathway for Anna Mae and Michael to chase the American dream. When Anna Mae was old enough to begin school in Olyphant, the nation had been plunged into the Great Depression. Wages for the minors were depressed, but the nation still ran on coal. The mine operated continuously throughout the Depression and Peter continued to earn a living wage, even if it was slimmer than he'd hoped for. Life in the company town revolved around work and church.

Workers living in a "company town" tended to move more than you might expect. There was an evolutionary aspect to moving. The newcomers ended up with the smallest houses. When they heard someone with a nicer house might be leaving, they put their names on the list asking for an "upgrade". Over time, a miner might go from a one-bedroom, to a two-bedroom, to a three-bedroom house. Moving wasn't as much of a sign of instability as it was a sign of upward mobility.

Saints Cyril and Methodius Ukrainian Catholic Church provided everything Pennsylvania Coal Company didn't. It moved into its massive new building in 1927 and counted about a thousand families as members of its parish. It was life's center for many of Ukrainian immigrants to Olyphant. It had a parish baseball team. Theater groups presented professional quality performances. It offered programs for the Boy Scouts. Although it didn't have a formal grade school, it did offer classes to help the immigrants learn English. It also had classes in Ukrainian so the immigrants' children could study the language of the homeland and learn about its history and culture.

Anna Mae and Michael started public school in Olyphant. They were both first generation "native born" Americans. Anna entered first-grade in 1934, Michael in 1936. They were pretty normal kids getting pretty normal grades, doing pretty normal things, and getting into normal trouble from time-to-time. They had no idea if they were rich or poor. They were coal miner's children just like most of the other kids in their classrooms. They had clothes on their backs. They had food on the table. Their world in the late 1930s was perfectly "normal" because they had but one standard to judge it against. It was the only world they knew.

Peter's world was a little more worrisome. He followed the stories in the newspaper about a Russian invasion of eastern Poland in 1939. The homeland he had left behind was at war yet again. By the first day of September, Hitler's troops bombarded Poland from the west. The Russians had the Ukraine; the Germans had Poland. The memories of Probizhna haunted Peter.

The political situation in Eastern Europe continued to degrade over the next year and a half. London was now being bombed on a nightly basis. Peter kept lugging coal by day and raising a family with Eva by night. But he watched and he worried. Then one late fall day in 1941, Peter's nightmare took a step closer to reality. On December 7, 1941, the Japanese bombed Pearl Harbor. The United States, the land to which Peter had come to escape the horrors of war, was itself at war.

News from "the front" dominated the news for the next three years. Michael had just entered the sixth grade when the 2nd World War broke loose. Like many of his first-generation American friends in school, he felt an ever-increasing surge of patriotism for his homeland. As he entered high school, his focus was squarely on what he could do to contribute to his country's efforts. When he was in 10th grade, World War Two came to an end. Rationing ended in Olyphant. Returning G.I.s brought a renewed vigor to Olyphant. Michael's patriotic spirit grew seemingly without bound. He knew what he wanted to do with his life and set his sights on that goal. The ink hadn't dried on his high school diploma when he enlisted in the United States Army.

Michael's first assignment after training was to join the U.S. occupation forces under the command of General Douglas MacArthur in Tokyo, Japan. He was discharged from the Army before he was twenty-one and joined the U.S. Air Force. He was sent to Germany and spent much of his six-year tour in Frankfort. Much of his time was spent coordinating and executing military transport systems. When he left the Air Force, he had attained the rank of Staff-Sergeant.

Chapter Five

Early in 1955, Michael passed through "The Valley of the Sun", also known as Phoenix, Arizona. In the dead of winter, he stood in the sun at Luke Air Force Base as the air massaged him with a gentle 78° breeze. He thought of the snows of Olyphant. He remembered the snows of Frankfurt, Germany. The memory of the icy winds of McGuire Air Force Base near Philadelphia made him shiver.

Michael was at a point in his life where he could reenlist in the Air Force and spend another six years on assignment in places that might not rank as the most desirable vacation spots on the planet or he could strike out on his own. Phoenix was a budding city with more than 100,000 residents in 1955. Phoenix Sky Harbor Airport had just opened and was one of the most modern and progressive airports in the nation. With his Air Force credentials, he knew he could get a good job in a heartbeat. He checked the weather report for the following day just to make sure he wasn't dreaming. His decision was made.

In January of 1956, Michael was a resident of Phoenix, Arizona. No longer on active duty with the Air Force, he had a commitment to the Reserves, but was looking forward to civilian life as a single, healthy, American male in paradise in the southwestern desert.

Before arriving, he discovered the Arizona National Guard had a spot for him as its chief cargomaster. Even though the Air National Guard was chartered and managed by the State of Arizona, it afforded Michael the opportunity to remain in the military, retain his Staff Sargeant rank and privilege, and best of all, stay in Arizona. He would spend the next 30 or so years with the Guard.

He was a dapper young man with bedroom eyes and a smile that could undress a marble statue of a princess. As a single man in a new town, Michael was driven to discover the haunts, meet some people, and otherwise learn how to become an Arizonan. He wasted no time in doing so.

When he learned the VFW had a social club not far from his apartment, he thought it might be a great way to relax, meet some other veterans, and socialize. On the twelfth day of May 1956, there was to be live music at the VFW. Michael wasn't scheduled to work the following day so it would be Saturday night at the VFW.

Michael arrived early (by young people's standards). The music wasn't to start until 9:00 p.m. Michael was sitting at the bar sipping on a cold beer when the band began its "mike check". A young woman walked into the hall and sat at a small table toward the end of the bar. She too began her Mike check. She noticed the good-looking young man sitting at the bar, but pretended to look away when he turned and spotted her. She sat alone. Michael assumed she was waiting for someone. What he didn't know was… she was waiting for him.

Monica was in a bad marriage with an abusive husband she had met when both were in the Air Force stationed in Texas. She had a son that wasn't yet two and, on that night, she had a babysitter. Her husband was out of town or so he told her. Michael ordered another beer.

When the band played *Rock around the* Clock for its second song, the dance floor began to fill with the Saturday night crowd. Mike noticed the young woman at the table was still without her guest. He approached her table and asked her if she'd like to shake a tail-feather with him. She was on her feet before Michael finished his question. They danced. The conversation flowed freely. Michael detected a hint of the South in her speech and learned she was Florida born and raised. When he learned she was a veteran of the Air Force, they had all the more in common. When he learned she was expecting no one else, Michael took his beer from the bar and joined her at the table. He bought her a beer. They talked and talked. There was chemistry at work as they shared their stories of life in the military.

He didn't want to seem too pushy, even though she pushed. He discovered her name was Monica, but didn't get her last name. They danced again. They both smoked Camel cigarettes at the table; another thing in common. As the evening wore on, they were enjoying themselves. On the slow dance, she pressed herself closer to Michael. Another beer, another dance. "The music is too loud to have a conversation," she said. He agreed.

"Why don't we leave and have a beer where it's not as loud." Michael had been around the world. He didn't need someone to explain what she meant. They left the dance together, but they danced well into the night. When they were about to go home, they embraced for a long time.

"I'd like to see you again. Can I call you?"

Monica replied, "I don't have a phone, but I come into the VFW from time-to-time. I'll see you again there."

They parted. Michael went home not knowing Monica's last name. Neither did he know she was married and had a toddler to tend. Nor did he know she was now pregnant. Monica went home to her unhappy house. She would never see Michael again.

On February 4th of 1957. Monica gave birth to Stephen William Hobgood, a strapping baby boy. Monica assumed her husband, Gerald, was the father, but she knew there were other possibilities. She vowed to keep her suspicions to herself. A year later, she had another child. The three boys were raised as if they were full brothers in a volatile home environment that was destined to fail within the next two years. Stephen wouldn't know for more than sixty-years that while he was the middle-child, he was the half-brother to the other two. Monica died in 1982 knowing she had three boys. She wanted to believe they shared the same father, but she knew better.

Michael met the girl of his dreams a couple years later and married Joan Stumpf in 1960. They were married for six years, but it was a tumultuous relationship. The dream turned into a nightmare and they divorced in 1967. There were no children involved, few assets to worry about, and not a bundle of great memories to share. They had married in their youths and as they grew, they grew in different directions. No harm – no foul. Game over.

(Michael is seen posing for a photo with Joan Stumpf in 1960.)

The now single Sargeant Polowy continued to perform well with the Air National Guard. The work ethic his father, Peter, had instilled in him served Michael well. He purchased a house in Phoenix, built friendships, and lived a good life. He remained single for the better part of the next seventeen years. Then he met the girl of his dreams. This time, however, it was the real deal. He married Martha Lou Weber on Valentine's Day of 1985. They would remain blissfully married until Marty died in 2007. They had a house in Scottsdale, another one in Apache Junction, and later, they purchased a summer home in Lakeside, Arizona, a small community in the pine forests of Arizona's White Mountains.

Until he died in the summer of 2019, Michael remained a friendly, gregarious, and special friend to many people who knew him. He loved to cook. He loved to fish. He loved his Ukrainian history. And he loved his family, even though he wasn't aware of how big it really was.

(Michael Polowy flashes his weaponized smile just before retiring from the Arizona Air National Guard.)

Chapter Six

The son Michael never knew he sired grew up in Phoenix, Arizona. Stephen Hobgood had no idea his real father was Michael Polowy. His presumed father, Gerald, was by all accounts, not a nice man. All three of boys could have used another father figure. Stephen could have had one if only his mother had known herself.

Young Stephen bore a strong resemblance to Michael. In later years, it would have become clear (had anyone know both Stephen and Michael) that you can't violate the laws of genetics. Stephen's smile was Michael's. Stephen's gregarious and friendly personality were gifted him by Michael. And like his father, Stephen had the bedroom eyes and the lethal smile that rendered the ladies helpless.

When Stephen was twenty-two, he had rented an apartment in south Scottsdale. One afternoon, there was a frantic knock on his door. He opened it to find the twenty-six-year-old woman who lived across the walk from him in a panic. "My water heater is leaking all over the floor," she stammered. "Can you help me?"

Stephen had a mechanical inclination and thought he'd at least give it a try. After all, it was the neighborly thing to do. Stephen went into Daphne's apartment and promptly plugged her leak. She thanked him generously. She gave him a hug that seemed disproportionate to the job he'd done. It soon became apparent there was more to the job than he had anticipated. Daphne's vocabulary may not have been the world's greatest, but one might have assumed she at least knew the definition of "No". Such was not the case.

Michael moved out of his apartment soon thereafter. Daphne also moved on. They never saw each other again. And like the father he never knew, Stephen was soon to be the father of a child he wouldn't know existed until forty years later.

Daphne was a free-spirit. No, I retract that. Daphne was just "free". She ended up having five children. If you count the suspects or potential fathers, she may be one of the few women to have five children by fourteen different fathers. The daughter sired by Michael's unknown son, Stephen, was the middle-child of Daphne's five. She was the only one of the five that was placed for adoption.

Many years later, we learned Daphne had placed the girl for adoption because the man she suspected as being the father was a hardened, violent criminal who to this day is incarcerated for violent sexual assaults. It's hard to know everything – if anything – that was going through Daphne's mind at the time, but she has sculpted her memories over the years to say she didn't want the predator father to have access to the child.

I have pretty extensive knowledge of this case because that adopted child's name is Tempest Jones. She is my daughter.

Tempest was brought to the White Mountains of Arizona to live with us when she was five-days-old. She was raised there, went to school there, and still has much of her adopted family living there. As she was growing up, we never tried to fool her into believing we were her birth parents. In fact, we always assured her that when she was "of age", if she wanted, we would do everything within our powers to help her find her birth family.

As her curiosity grew, she had questions. "Why did my birth mother give me up?" She seemed to be trying to deal with some kind of "rejection". What was wrong with her that would cause a mother to reject her? We decided it was time to have a lengthier, more in-depth discussion with Tempest on the matter.

It was a Sunday in late October in 1995. The weather was perfect. Hints of fall colors lingered on the trees. We packed a picnic lunch and decided to visit Fred's Lake, just up the road from our home. We thought the peace and quiet of nature viewed from a small boat on a serene lake would be conducive to a potentially heavy discussion of such matters. Tempest was fifteen. We packed a picnic lunch, grabbed our fishing poles and headed out. First, we had to stop at Walmart to pick up some fish hooks, lurers, and other angler supplies. When we got to the counter, the clerk was already waiting on a white-haired man, but we patiently waited. When he finished his transaction, he wheeled around to leave and accidentally bumped into Tempest. He apologized with such a warm smile, we almost felt guilty just standing there. He looked Tempest in the eyes and said, "Are you going fishing today? What's your name?"

"Yes, we're going to Fred's Lake. I'm Tempest Jones," she replied.

"Well, please forgive me," he said. "I'm going fishing today too. It's my birthday. I'm Mike Polowy." He held out his hand. Tempest shook it and mirrored his smile. They almost looked alike.

When Tempest turned nineteen, she asked for that help. It took us a couple years, but we finally found her birth mother, Daphne. A meeting was arranged. Tempest would finally have some roots, at least on her maternal side.

When Tempest and Daphne met, Tempest was anxious to learn about her family history. Imagine her shock when Daphne told her, "I too was adopted. I have no idea who my real parents are."

Everyone was shocked. To make matters worse, Daphne insisted she didn't remember the father's name, so that roadblock remained. However, we doggedly persisted. My wife and I both took classes in genealogy and genetics. We took classes through State of Arizona with the intent of becoming "Confidential Intermediaries", a small group of investigators licensed by the State to (among other things) open the private files of adoptees in search of their birth parents.

With a combination of hard work over the course of ten years, we located the man who was identified on the original birth certificate as the father. When confronted, Daphne admitted that he was the culprit. He was difficult to locate because he had changed his name and then was sentenced to what was effectively life in prison. As the final step in confirming his identity, I arranged for a visit to the maximum-security section of one of Arizona's prisons.

As it happened, the man obviously had some serious mental issues and the veracity of his claims was more than suspect. However, he remembered enough about the events of the time to make us believe he was our guy. We even went to the effort of building an extensive family tree and presenting it to Tempest.

The house of cards began to collapse when we found his brother, a respected optometrist in the Seattle area. He agreed to take a DNA test. Things didn't line up the way they were presumed. The convict wasn't the father.

We approached Daphne and finally got her to agree to a DNA test. Between her test results and those from Tempest herself, we were able to separate relatives into two groups, one of Daphne's relatives, the other containing the relations of Tempest's actual birth father – whoever he might be.

With countless hours of work and some very sophisticated tools for DNA analysis, the puzzle pieces started coming together. We kept tightening the circle until things started pointing toward a man named Stephen Hobgood. The road to that conclusion was full of potholes and traps. For example, the discovery that

Stephen was the middle child of three, but didn't share a father with them. That rocked a few minds and raised two questions for every one answered.

We were elated that it appeared we had solved a twenty-year-old mystery. We contacted Daphne and asked her, "Is it possible that a man named Stephen Hobgood is the father of Tempest?"

Daphne with almost joy in her voice said, "Oh yea! I forgot about him. I guess it could be. I hope it is; he was a really nice guy."

We were stunned to learn Stephen had fathered other children. Tempest has a half-brother living just a few miles away who shares Stephen as a father, but has a different mother. Stephen was not aware of the existence of either of these children.

Nonetheless, the evidence gradually became overwhelming. So, let me be perfectly clear:

> Tempest is the unknown daughter of a man (Stephen) who is the unknown son of a man (Michael) who is the son of a man (Peter) from an unknown country called the Ukraine or Poland or Galicia or Austria or Russia or Disneyland. She is not the daughter of the violent rapist who is rotting away in prison. In a nutshell, Tempest is the great granddaughter of Peter Polowy who is from Prohizhna. Is it all clear now?

That's the story of how we got to know Peter Polowy. He had to be a great guy because he overcame more hardship than most people can ever imagine. And then… He produced a wonderful family.

(From left to right, taken the day they first met: Stephen Hobgood, previously unknown son, Garrick Henry, and previously unknown daughter, Tempest Jones. Taken at the family "union". It wasn't a "reunion" because that term suggests getting together again. This was the first time they had every met face-to-face.)

Gratitude and Credits to:

Linda (Polowy) Novak for her invaluable contributions to the story.

Greggory Novak for answering the door.

Eugene Maslar – Olyphant, Pennsylvania and Ukrainian historian.

Sandra Walker – Warden, Wilmot Correctional Facility, for violating every rule in the book and allowing us to visit a dangerous prisoner without pre-authorization.

Professor Natalia Nowakowska, Oxford University, England for introducing me to…

Roger Moorhouse, one of the world's foremost experts on the history the Ukrainian-Polish history around the turn of the 20th century. He provided me with incredible insights into the history of the Polish Blue Army.

Armin "Chip" Rade, half-brother of Stephen Hobgood, for the invaluable assistance in solving the very complex mystery.

The Pulaski Club of Phoenix for providing translators and top-notch kielbasa and perogies.

Countless Polowy family members too numerous to mention who responded to my endless queries in my search for answers.

And especially, Stephen Hobgood for traveling coast-to-coast to surprise and hug the family he had never known.

About the Author

h. Alton Jones is a native of Detroit, Michigan. He is a "High Honors" graduate of Michigan State University where he attended undergraduate and graduate school in chemical engineering. He studied for his Ph.D. at the University of Arizona in Tucson. He began his writing and reporting career in Ann Arbor, Michigan in 1966 and worked in the broadcast news industry in Detroit, Denver, Miami and Portland, Oregon. After leaving the news business to found and operate a successful software company, he returned to the media world in 2000 writing a regular column in an Arizona newspaper for nearly ten years. He is the author of a number of books including *The Man on the Bench*. Together with his wife of nearly forty years, Liz McCarty, he still travels the world seeking adventure and new horizons. When not travelling, he lives in Scottsdale, Arizona.

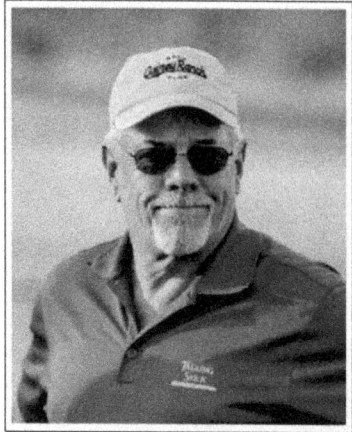

Other Books by h. Alton Jones
> The Man on the Bench (www.TheManOnTheBench.com)
> How to Cheat Golf
> Widow's Peak (with Liz McCarty)
> Searching for Dunderhead